This Book Belongs To:

....

....

....

....

WEBSITE

LOGIN

PASSWORD

NOTES

WEBSITE

LOGIN

PASSWORD

NOTES

WEBSITE

LOGIN

PASSWORD

NOTES

WEBSITE

LOGIN

PASSWORD

NOTES

WEBSITE

LOGIN

PASSWORD

NOTES

WEBSITE

LOGIN

PASSWORD

NOTES

WEBSITE

LOGIN

PASSWORD

NOTES

WEBSITE

LOGIN

PASSWORD

NOTES

WEBSITE

LOGIN

PASSWORD

NOTES

WEBSITE

LOGIN

PASSWORD

NOTES

WEBSITE

LOGIN

PASSWORD

NOTES

WEBSITE

LOGIN

PASSWORD

NOTES

WEBSITE

LOGIN

PASSWORD

NOTES

WEBSITE

LOGIN

PASSWORD

NOTES

WEBSITE

LOGIN

PASSWORD

NOTES

WEBSITE

LOGIN

PASSWORD

NOTES

WEBSITE

LOGIN

PASSWORD

NOTES

WEBSITE

LOGIN

PASSWORD

NOTES

WEBSITE

LOGIN

PASSWORD

NOTES

WEBSITE

LOGIN

PASSWORD

NOTES

WEBSITE

LOGIN

PASSWORD

NOTES

WEBSITE

LOGIN

PASSWORD

NOTES

WEBSITE

LOGIN

PASSWORD

NOTES

WEBSITE

LOGIN

PASSWORD

NOTES

WEBSITE

LOGIN

PASSWORD

NOTES

WEBSITE

LOGIN

PASSWORD

NOTES

WEBSITE

LOGIN

PASSWORD

NOTES

WEBSITE

LOGIN

PASSWORD

NOTES

WEBSITE

LOGIN

PASSWORD

NOTES

WEBSITE

LOGIN

PASSWORD

NOTES

WEBSITE

LOGIN

PASSWORD

NOTES

WEBSITE

LOGIN

PASSWORD

NOTES

WEBSITE

LOGIN

PASSWORD

NOTES

WEBSITE

LOGIN

PASSWORD

NOTES

WEBSITE

LOGIN

PASSWORD

NOTES

WEBSITE

LOGIN

PASSWORD

NOTES

WEBSITE

LOGIN

PASSWORD

NOTES

WEBSITE

LOGIN

PASSWORD

NOTES

WEBSITE

LOGIN

PASSWORD

NOTES

WEBSITE

LOGIN

PASSWORD

NOTES

WEBSITE

LOGIN

PASSWORD

NOTES

WEBSITE

LOGIN

PASSWORD

NOTES

WEBSITE

LOGIN

PASSWORD

NOTES

WEBSITE

LOGIN

PASSWORD

NOTES

WEBSITE

LOGIN

PASSWORD

NOTES

WEBSITE

LOGIN

PASSWORD

NOTES

WEBSITE

LOGIN

PASSWORD

NOTES

WEBSITE

LOGIN

PASSWORD

NOTES

WEBSITE

LOGIN

PASSWORD

NOTES

WEBSITE

LOGIN

PASSWORD

NOTES

WEBSITE

LOGIN

PASSWORD

NOTES

WEBSITE

LOGIN

PASSWORD

NOTES

WEBSITE

LOGIN

PASSWORD

NOTES

WEBSITE

LOGIN

PASSWORD

NOTES

WEBSITE

LOGIN

PASSWORD

NOTES

WEBSITE

LOGIN

PASSWORD

NOTES

WEBSITE

LOGIN

PASSWORD

NOTES

WEBSITE

LOGIN

PASSWORD

NOTES

WEBSITE

LOGIN

PASSWORD

NOTES

WEBSITE

LOGIN

PASSWORD

NOTES

D

WEBSITE

LOGIN

PASSWORD

NOTES

WEBSITE

LOGIN

PASSWORD

NOTES

WEBSITE

LOGIN

PASSWORD

NOTES

WEBSITE

LOGIN

PASSWORD

NOTES

WEBSITE

LOGIN

PASSWORD

NOTES

WEBSITE

LOGIN

PASSWORD

NOTES

WEBSITE

LOGIN

PASSWORD

NOTES

WEBSITE

LOGIN

PASSWORD

NOTES

WEBSITE

LOGIN

PASSWORD

NOTES

WEBSITE

LOGIN

PASSWORD

NOTES

WEBSITE

LOGIN

PASSWORD

NOTES

WEBSITE

LOGIN

PASSWORD

NOTES

WEBSITE

LOGIN

PASSWORD

NOTES

WEBSITE

LOGIN

PASSWORD

NOTES

WEBSITE

LOGIN

PASSWORD

NOTES

WEBSITE

LOGIN

PASSWORD

NOTES

WEBSITE

LOGIN

PASSWORD

NOTES

WEBSITE

LOGIN

PASSWORD

NOTES

WEBSITE

LOGIN

PASSWORD

NOTES

WEBSITE

LOGIN

PASSWORD

NOTES

WEBSITE

LOGIN

PASSWORD

NOTES

WEBSITE

LOGIN

PASSWORD

NOTES

WEBSITE

LOGIN

PASSWORD

NOTES

WEBSITE

LOGIN

PASSWORD

NOTES

WEBSITE

LOGIN

PASSWORD

NOTES

WEBSITE

LOGIN

PASSWORD

NOTES

WEBSITE

LOGIN

PASSWORD

NOTES

WEBSITE

LOGIN

PASSWORD

NOTES

WEBSITE

LOGIN

PASSWORD

NOTES

WEBSITE

LOGIN

PASSWORD

NOTES

WEBSITE

LOGIN

PASSWORD

NOTES

WEBSITE

LOGIN

PASSWORD

NOTES

WEBSITE

LOGIN

PASSWORD

NOTES

WEBSITE

LOGIN

PASSWORD

NOTES

WEBSITE

LOGIN

PASSWORD

NOTES

WEBSITE

LOGIN

PASSWORD

NOTES

WEBSITE

LOGIN

PASSWORD

NOTES

WEBSITE

LOGIN

PASSWORD

NOTES

WEBSITE

LOGIN

PASSWORD

NOTES

WEBSITE

LOGIN

PASSWORD

NOTES

WEBSITE

LOGIN

PASSWORD

NOTES

WEBSITE

LOGIN

PASSWORD

NOTES

WEBSITE

LOGIN

PASSWORD

NOTES

WEBSITE

LOGIN

PASSWORD

NOTES

WEBSITE

LOGIN

PASSWORD

NOTES

WEBSITE

LOGIN

PASSWORD

NOTES

WEBSITE

LOGIN

PASSWORD

NOTES

WEBSITE

LOGIN

PASSWORD

NOTES

WEBSITE

LOGIN

PASSWORD

NOTES

WEBSITE

LOGIN

PASSWORD

NOTES

WEBSITE

LOGIN

PASSWORD

NOTES

WEBSITE

LOGIN

PASSWORD

NOTES

WEBSITE

LOGIN

PASSWORD

NOTES

WEBSITE

LOGIN

PASSWORD

NOTES

WEBSITE

LOGIN

PASSWORD

NOTES

WEBSITE

LOGIN

PASSWORD

NOTES

WEBSITE

LOGIN

PASSWORD

NOTES

WEBSITE

LOGIN

PASSWORD

NOTES

WEBSITE

LOGIN

PASSWORD

NOTES

WEBSITE

LOGIN

PASSWORD

NOTES

WEBSITE

LOGIN

PASSWORD

NOTES

WEBSITE

LOGIN

PASSWORD

NOTES

WEBSITE

LOGIN

PASSWORD

NOTES

WEBSITE

LOGIN

PASSWORD

NOTES

WEBSITE

LOGIN

PASSWORD

NOTES

WEBSITE

LOGIN

PASSWORD

NOTES

WEBSITE

LOGIN

PASSWORD

NOTES

WEBSITE

LOGIN

PASSWORD

NOTES

WEBSITE

LOGIN

PASSWORD

NOTES

WEBSITE

LOGIN

PASSWORD

NOTES

WEBSITE

LOGIN

PASSWORD

NOTES

WEBSITE

LOGIN

PASSWORD

NOTES

WEBSITE

LOGIN

PASSWORD

NOTES

WEBSITE

LOGIN

PASSWORD

NOTES

WEBSITE

LOGIN

PASSWORD

NOTES

WEBSITE

LOGIN

PASSWORD

NOTES

WEBSITE

LOGIN

PASSWORD

NOTES

WEBSITE

LOGIN

PASSWORD

NOTES

WEBSITE

LOGIN

PASSWORD

NOTES

WEBSITE

LOGIN

PASSWORD

NOTES

WEBSITE

LOGIN

PASSWORD

NOTES

WEBSITE

LOGIN

PASSWORD

NOTES

WEBSITE

LOGIN

PASSWORD

NOTES

WEBSITE

LOGIN

PASSWORD

NOTES

WEBSITE

LOGIN

PASSWORD

NOTES

WEBSITE

LOGIN

PASSWORD

NOTES

WEBSITE

LOGIN

PASSWORD

NOTES

WEBSITE

LOGIN

PASSWORD

NOTES

WEBSITE

LOGIN

PASSWORD

NOTES

WEBSITE

LOGIN

PASSWORD

NOTES

WEBSITE

LOGIN

PASSWORD

NOTES

WEBSITE

LOGIN

PASSWORD

NOTES

WEBSITE

LOGIN

PASSWORD

NOTES

WEBSITE

LOGIN

PASSWORD

NOTES

WEBSITE

LOGIN

PASSWORD

NOTES

WEBSITE

LOGIN

PASSWORD

NOTES

WEBSITE

LOGIN

PASSWORD

NOTES

WEBSITE

LOGIN

PASSWORD

NOTES

WEBSITE

LOGIN

PASSWORD

NOTES

WEBSITE

LOGIN

PASSWORD

NOTES

WEBSITE

LOGIN

PASSWORD

NOTES

WEBSITE

LOGIN

PASSWORD

NOTES

WEBSITE

LOGIN

PASSWORD

NOTES

WEBSITE

LOGIN

PASSWORD

NOTES

WEBSITE

LOGIN

PASSWORD

NOTES

WEBSITE

LOGIN

PASSWORD

NOTES

WEBSITE

LOGIN

PASSWORD

NOTES

WEBSITE

LOGIN

PASSWORD

NOTES

WEBSITE

LOGIN

PASSWORD

NOTES

WEBSITE

LOGIN

PASSWORD

NOTES

WEBSITE

LOGIN

PASSWORD

NOTES

WEBSITE

LOGIN

PASSWORD

NOTES

WEBSITE

LOGIN

PASSWORD

NOTES

WEBSITE

LOGIN

PASSWORD

NOTES

WEBSITE

LOGIN

PASSWORD

NOTES

WEBSITE

LOGIN

PASSWORD

NOTES

WEBSITE

LOGIN

PASSWORD

NOTES

WEBSITE

LOGIN

PASSWORD

NOTES

WEBSITE

LOGIN

PASSWORD

NOTES

WEBSITE

LOGIN

PASSWORD

NOTES

WEBSITE

LOGIN

PASSWORD

NOTES

WEBSITE

LOGIN

PASSWORD

NOTES

WEBSITE

LOGIN

PASSWORD

NOTES

WEBSITE

LOGIN

PASSWORD

NOTES

WEBSITE

LOGIN

PASSWORD

NOTES

WEBSITE

LOGIN

PASSWORD

NOTES

WEBSITE

LOGIN

PASSWORD

NOTES

WEBSITE

LOGIN

PASSWORD

NOTES

WEBSITE

LOGIN

PASSWORD

NOTES

WEBSITE

LOGIN

PASSWORD

NOTES

WEBSITE

LOGIN

PASSWORD

NOTES

WEBSITE

LOGIN

PASSWORD

NOTES

WEBSITE

LOGIN

PASSWORD

NOTES

WEBSITE

LOGIN

PASSWORD

NOTES

WEBSITE

LOGIN

PASSWORD

NOTES

WEBSITE

LOGIN

PASSWORD

NOTES

WEBSITE

LOGIN

PASSWORD

NOTES

WEBSITE

LOGIN

PASSWORD

NOTES

WEBSITE

LOGIN

PASSWORD

NOTES

WEBSITE

LOGIN

PASSWORD

NOTES

WEBSITE

LOGIN

PASSWORD

NOTES

WEBSITE

LOGIN

PASSWORD

NOTES

WEBSITE

LOGIN

PASSWORD

NOTES

WEBSITE

LOGIN

PASSWORD

NOTES

WEBSITE

LOGIN

PASSWORD

NOTES

WEBSITE

LOGIN

PASSWORD

NOTES

WEBSITE

LOGIN

PASSWORD

NOTES

WEBSITE

LOGIN

PASSWORD

NOTES

WEBSITE

LOGIN

PASSWORD

NOTES

WEBSITE

LOGIN

PASSWORD

NOTES

WEBSITE

LOGIN

PASSWORD

NOTES

WEBSITE

LOGIN

PASSWORD

NOTES

WEBSITE

LOGIN

PASSWORD

NOTES

WEBSITE

LOGIN

PASSWORD

NOTES

WEBSITE

LOGIN

PASSWORD

NOTES

WEBSITE

LOGIN

PASSWORD

NOTES

WEBSITE

LOGIN

PASSWORD

NOTES

WEBSITE

LOGIN

PASSWORD

NOTES

WEBSITE

LOGIN

PASSWORD

NOTES

WEBSITE

LOGIN

PASSWORD

NOTES

WEBSITE

LOGIN

PASSWORD

NOTES

WEBSITE

LOGIN

PASSWORD

NOTES

WEBSITE

LOGIN

PASSWORD

NOTES

WEBSITE

LOGIN

PASSWORD

NOTES

WEBSITE

LOGIN

PASSWORD

NOTES

WEBSITE

LOGIN

PASSWORD

NOTES

WEBSITE

LOGIN

PASSWORD

NOTES

WEBSITE

LOGIN

PASSWORD

NOTES

WEBSITE

LOGIN

PASSWORD

NOTES

WEBSITE

LOGIN

PASSWORD

NOTES

WEBSITE

LOGIN

PASSWORD

NOTES

WEBSITE

LOGIN

PASSWORD

NOTES

WEBSITE

LOGIN

PASSWORD

NOTES

WEBSITE

LOGIN

PASSWORD

NOTES

WEBSITE

LOGIN

PASSWORD

NOTES

WEBSITE

LOGIN

PASSWORD

NOTES

WEBSITE

LOGIN

PASSWORD

NOTES

WEBSITE

LOGIN

PASSWORD

NOTES

WEBSITE

LOGIN

PASSWORD

NOTES

WEBSITE

LOGIN

PASSWORD

NOTES

WEBSITE

LOGIN

PASSWORD

NOTES

WEBSITE

LOGIN

PASSWORD

NOTES

WEBSITE

LOGIN

PASSWORD

NOTES

WEBSITE

LOGIN

PASSWORD

NOTES

WEBSITE

LOGIN

PASSWORD

NOTES

WEBSITE

LOGIN

PASSWORD

NOTES

WEBSITE

LOGIN

PASSWORD

NOTES

WEBSITE

LOGIN

PASSWORD

NOTES

WEBSITE

LOGIN

PASSWORD

NOTES

WEBSITE

LOGIN

PASSWORD

NOTES

WEBSITE

LOGIN

PASSWORD

NOTES

WEBSITE

LOGIN

PASSWORD

NOTES

WEBSITE

LOGIN

PASSWORD

NOTES

WEBSITE

LOGIN

PASSWORD

NOTES

WEBSITE

LOGIN

PASSWORD

NOTES

WEBSITE

LOGIN

PASSWORD

NOTES

WEBSITE

LOGIN

PASSWORD

NOTES

WEBSITE

LOGIN

PASSWORD

NOTES

WEBSITE

LOGIN

PASSWORD

NOTES

WEBSITE

LOGIN

PASSWORD

NOTES

WEBSITE

LOGIN

PASSWORD

NOTES

WEBSITE

LOGIN

PASSWORD

NOTES

WEBSITE

LOGIN

PASSWORD

NOTES

WEBSITE

LOGIN

PASSWORD

NOTES

WEBSITE

LOGIN

PASSWORD

NOTES

WEBSITE

LOGIN

PASSWORD

NOTES

WEBSITE

LOGIN

PASSWORD

NOTES

WEBSITE

LOGIN

PASSWORD

NOTES

WEBSITE

LOGIN

PASSWORD

NOTES

WEBSITE

LOGIN

PASSWORD

NOTES

WEBSITE

LOGIN

PASSWORD

NOTES

WEBSITE

LOGIN

PASSWORD

NOTES

WEBSITE

LOGIN

PASSWORD

NOTES

WEBSITE

LOGIN

PASSWORD

NOTES

WEBSITE

LOGIN

PASSWORD

NOTES

WEBSITE

LOGIN

PASSWORD

NOTES

WEBSITE

LOGIN

PASSWORD

NOTES

WEBSITE

LOGIN

PASSWORD

NOTES

WEBSITE

LOGIN

PASSWORD

NOTES

WEBSITE

LOGIN

PASSWORD

NOTES

WEBSITE

LOGIN

PASSWORD

NOTES

WEBSITE

LOGIN

PASSWORD

NOTES

WEBSITE

LOGIN

PASSWORD

NOTES

WEBSITE

LOGIN

PASSWORD

NOTES

WEBSITE

LOGIN

PASSWORD

NOTES

WEBSITE

LOGIN

PASSWORD

NOTES

WEBSITE

LOGIN

PASSWORD

NOTES

WEBSITE

LOGIN

PASSWORD

NOTES

WEBSITE

LOGIN

PASSWORD

NOTES

WEBSITE

LOGIN

PASSWORD

NOTES

WEBSITE

LOGIN

PASSWORD

NOTES

WEBSITE

LOGIN

PASSWORD

NOTES

WEBSITE

LOGIN

PASSWORD

NOTES

WEBSITE

LOGIN

PASSWORD

NOTES

WEBSITE

LOGIN

PASSWORD

NOTES

WEBSITE

LOGIN

PASSWORD

NOTES

WEBSITE

LOGIN

PASSWORD

NOTES

WEBSITE

LOGIN

PASSWORD

NOTES

WEBSITE

LOGIN

PASSWORD

NOTES

WEBSITE

LOGIN

PASSWORD

NOTES

WEBSITE

LOGIN

PASSWORD

NOTES

WEBSITE

LOGIN

PASSWORD

NOTES

WEBSITE

LOGIN

PASSWORD

NOTES

WEBSITE

LOGIN

PASSWORD

NOTES

WEBSITE

LOGIN

PASSWORD

NOTES

WEBSITE

LOGIN

PASSWORD

NOTES

WEBSITE

LOGIN

PASSWORD

NOTES

WEBSITE

LOGIN

PASSWORD

NOTES

WEBSITE

LOGIN

PASSWORD

NOTES

WEBSITE

LOGIN

PASSWORD

NOTES

WEBSITE

LOGIN

PASSWORD

NOTES

WEBSITE

LOGIN

PASSWORD

NOTES

WEBSITE

LOGIN

PASSWORD

NOTES

WEBSITE

LOGIN

PASSWORD

NOTES

WEBSITE

LOGIN

PASSWORD

NOTES

WEBSITE

LOGIN

PASSWORD

NOTES

WEBSITE

LOGIN

PASSWORD

NOTES

WEBSITE

LOGIN

PASSWORD

NOTES

WEBSITE

LOGIN

PASSWORD

NOTES

WEBSITE

LOGIN

PASSWORD

NOTES

WEBSITE

LOGIN

PASSWORD

NOTES

WEBSITE

LOGIN

PASSWORD

NOTES

WEBSITE

LOGIN

PASSWORD

NOTES

WEBSITE

LOGIN

PASSWORD

NOTES

WEBSITE

LOGIN

PASSWORD

NOTES

WEBSITE

LOGIN

PASSWORD

NOTES

WEBSITE

LOGIN

PASSWORD

NOTES

WEBSITE

LOGIN

PASSWORD

NOTES

WEBSITE

LOGIN

PASSWORD

NOTES

WEBSITE

LOGIN

PASSWORD

NOTES

WEBSITE

LOGIN

PASSWORD

NOTES

WEBSITE

LOGIN

PASSWORD

NOTES

WEBSITE

LOGIN

PASSWORD

NOTES

WEBSITE

LOGIN

PASSWORD

NOTES

WEBSITE

LOGIN

PASSWORD

NOTES

WEBSITE

LOGIN

PASSWORD

NOTES

WEBSITE

LOGIN

PASSWORD

NOTES

WEBSITE

LOGIN

PASSWORD

NOTES

WEBSITE

LOGIN

PASSWORD

NOTES

WEBSITE

LOGIN

PASSWORD

NOTES

WEBSITE

LOGIN

PASSWORD

NOTES

WEBSITE

LOGIN

PASSWORD

NOTES

WEBSITE

LOGIN

PASSWORD

NOTES

WEBSITE

LOGIN

PASSWORD

NOTES

WEBSITE

LOGIN

PASSWORD

NOTES

WEBSITE

LOGIN

PASSWORD

NOTES

WEBSITE

LOGIN

PASSWORD

NOTES

WEBSITE

LOGIN

PASSWORD

NOTES

WEBSITE

LOGIN

PASSWORD

NOTES

WEBSITE

LOGIN

PASSWORD

NOTES

WEBSITE

LOGIN

PASSWORD

NOTES

WEBSITE

LOGIN

PASSWORD

NOTES

WEBSITE

LOGIN

PASSWORD

NOTES

WEBSITE

LOGIN

PASSWORD

NOTES

WEBSITE

LOGIN

PASSWORD

NOTES

WEBSITE

LOGIN

PASSWORD

NOTES

WEBSITE

LOGIN

PASSWORD

NOTES

WEBSITE

LOGIN

PASSWORD

NOTES

WEBSITE

LOGIN

PASSWORD

NOTES

WEBSITE

LOGIN

PASSWORD

NOTES

WEBSITE

LOGIN

PASSWORD

NOTES

WEBSITE

LOGIN

PASSWORD

NOTES

WEBSITE

LOGIN

PASSWORD

NOTES

WEBSITE

LOGIN

PASSWORD

NOTES

WEBSITE

LOGIN

PASSWORD

NOTES

WEBSITE

LOGIN

PASSWORD

NOTES

WEBSITE

LOGIN

PASSWORD

NOTES

WEBSITE

LOGIN

PASSWORD

NOTES

WEBSITE

LOGIN

PASSWORD

NOTES

WEBSITE

LOGIN

PASSWORD

NOTES

WEBSITE

LOGIN

PASSWORD

NOTES

WEBSITE

LOGIN

PASSWORD

NOTES

WEBSITE

LOGIN

PASSWORD

NOTES

WEBSITE

LOGIN

PASSWORD

NOTES

WEBSITE

LOGIN

PASSWORD

NOTES

WEBSITE

LOGIN

PASSWORD

NOTES

WEBSITE

LOGIN

PASSWORD

NOTES

WEBSITE

LOGIN

PASSWORD

NOTES

WEBSITE

LOGIN

PASSWORD

NOTES

WEBSITE

LOGIN

PASSWORD

NOTES

WEBSITE

LOGIN

PASSWORD

NOTES

WEBSITE

LOGIN

PASSWORD

NOTES

WEBSITE

LOGIN

PASSWORD

NOTES

WEBSITE

LOGIN

PASSWORD

NOTES

WEBSITE

LOGIN

PASSWORD

NOTES

WEBSITE

LOGIN

PASSWORD

NOTES

WEBSITE

LOGIN

PASSWORD

NOTES

WEBSITE

LOGIN

PASSWORD

NOTES

WEBSITE

LOGIN

PASSWORD

NOTES

WEBSITE

LOGIN

PASSWORD

NOTES

WEBSITE

LOGIN

PASSWORD

NOTES

WEBSITE

LOGIN

PASSWORD

NOTES

WEBSITE

LOGIN

PASSWORD

NOTES

WEBSITE

LOGIN

PASSWORD

NOTES

WEBSITE

LOGIN

PASSWORD

NOTES

WEBSITE

LOGIN

PASSWORD

NOTES

WEBSITE

LOGIN

PASSWORD

NOTES

WEBSITE

LOGIN

PASSWORD

NOTES

WEBSITE

LOGIN

PASSWORD

NOTES

WEBSITE

LOGIN

PASSWORD

NOTES

WEBSITE
LOGIN
PASSWORD
NOTES

WEBSITE
LOGIN
PASSWORD
NOTES

WEBSITE
LOGIN
PASSWORD
NOTES

WEBSITE
LOGIN
PASSWORD
NOTES

WEBSITE

LOGIN

PASSWORD

NOTES

WEBSITE

LOGIN

PASSWORD

NOTES

WEBSITE

LOGIN

PASSWORD

NOTES

WEBSITE

LOGIN

PASSWORD

NOTES

WEBSITE

LOGIN

PASSWORD

NOTES

WEBSITE

LOGIN

PASSWORD

NOTES

WEBSITE

LOGIN

PASSWORD

NOTES

WEBSITE

LOGIN

PASSWORD

NOTES

WEBSITE

LOGIN

PASSWORD

NOTES

WEBSITE

LOGIN

PASSWORD

NOTES

WEBSITE

LOGIN

PASSWORD

NOTES

WEBSITE

LOGIN

PASSWORD

NOTES